YOUR KNOWLEDGE HAS VALUE

Nicola Gundrum

The Marketing Strategy of the foreign Hypermarket Wal-Mart in China

Is Wal-Mart's Marketing Strategy adapted to the Chinese Market?

GRIN Verlag

Bibliografische Information der Deutschen Nationalbibliothek:

Die Deutsche Bibliothek verzeichnet diese Publikation in der Deutschen National-
bibliografie; detaillierte bibliografische Daten sind im Internet über http://dnb.d-
nb.de/ abrufbar.

Imprint:

Copyright © 2011 GRIN Verlag GmbH
Druck und Bindung: Books on Demand GmbH, Norderstedt Germany
ISBN: 978-3-656-30082-3

GRIN - Your knowledge has value

Der GRIN Verlag publiziert seit 1998 wissenschaftliche Arbeiten von Studenten, Hochschullehrern und anderen Akademikern als eBook und gedrucktes Buch. Die Verlagswebsite www.grin.com ist die ideale Plattform zur Veröffentlichung von Hausarbeiten, Abschlussarbeiten, wissenschaftlichen Aufsätzen, Dissertationen und Fachbüchern.

Shanghai University
Assignment

Area of expertise: Marketing China

Topic: The Marketing Strategy of the foreign Hypermarket Wal-Mart in China

Is Wal-Mart's marketing strategy adapted to the Chinese market?

Submitted by: Nicola Gundrum

Submitted on: 13 May 2011

The Marketing Strategy of the foreign Hypermarket Wal-Mart in China

Introduction of China's hypermarket industry:

Hypermarkets are taking hold in China because of the lure of low prices, convenient one-stop shopping, accessible locations and the integration of facilities such as restaurants, cinemas and coffee shops. And experts predict there are further opportunities for hypermarket growth in smaller cities all over China. They say that the one-stop shop philosophy is more and more attracting the attention of middle-class consumers, the largest spenders in China. Every ten days the middle-class consumers in China visit hypermarkets.[1]

Market Structure:

In 2003 Chinese consumers spend as a whole 9.2 trillion RMB. 41 percent of that was invested in food - a decline of 7 percent compared to the year 1997 and the simultaneous expression of a transformation to a modern consumption structure. The sharp increase of the consumer spending overall by 64.2 percent since 1997 is due mainly to the high economic growth of 9 percent annually. Therefore the household income rose steadily from 1997 to 2003.[2]

The Chinese hypermarket sector is still stuck in transition. Chinese supermarket chains have also not a decade-long experience like similar companies in Europe because there were not any private supermarkets in China until the mid-90s. There were almost only national department stores and small independent shops and street markets. They are not (yet) represented all over the country, but they grow fast.[3]

[1] Chaudhrey, R. (2007).
[2] Wesnitzer, A. (2005).
[3] Wesnitzer, A. (2005).

Market demand:

Studies state that from the year 2005 to 2006 hypermarkets increased their value share of China's grocery sector in the 15 largest cities of the country from 28.5% to 29.8%. The share in these big provincial capital cities and municipalities – called tier one cities – has continued to increase and reached 30.1% in the first half of 2007. At the end of the decade the share of the hypermarkets was 35%.[1]

The hypermarket success interacts with the supermarket sector, however, which has recently experienced retrenchment. The supermarket value share has decreased from 28.4% in 2001 to 19.1% in the first half of 2007. The number of visits consumers make each year to hypermarkets have risen since 2005, while visits to supermarkets has been dropped over the same period. Till now, hypermarkets had made their biggest impact in Shanghai. They have a 45% value share. Hypermarkets have also a huge influence in Hangzhou (37.9%) and Shenzhen (37.2%).[2]

Main players & competitions:

The one hundred largest hypermarkets in China achieved total sales of nearly 1.4 trillion RMB in the year 2009. This represents an increase compared to the previous year by 13.5%. Among the ten largest retailers were only four foreigners like last year: RT-Mart, Carrefour, Wal-Mart and Taiwan's RT-Mart. Their market shares range between 2.2% (RT-Mart) and 4.7% (Wal-Mart) in the 15 largest cities of China.[3] Not long time ago, for instance, Carrefour opened its 100th hypermarket in China in Shaoxing, a comparative small Chinese city with a population of 650,000.[4] The largest German representative is the Metro Group, which however could not keep up with the expanding market. Revenues decreased 5% to 12.0 billion Yuan, and the company slipped down in the ranking by seven places and ranks now at the 31st position. IKEA improved much more favorable, which sales rose 16% to 3.1 billion Yuan.[5]

[1] **Chaudhrey, R.** (2007).
[2] **Chaudhrey, R.** (2007).
[3] **Schaaf, B.** (2010).
[4] **Chaudhrey, R.** (2007).
[5] **Schaaf, B.** (2010).

The gained revenues show how strong fragmented the Chinese retail market still is. Less than 25% of the proceeds of the hundreds of major retailers account for Suning, Gome or Bailian. In terms of total retail trade (including cars, pharmacies, etc.), there are even much less. China's largest retailer - Suning - In 2009, revenues in the amount equivalent to only 17.1 billion U.S. $, while, for example Metro realized worldwide with $ 91.4 billion over five times as much.[1]

OBI has however given up its business in China and the main rival B&Q bought the company. The discount supermarket Plus, owned by the international trade chain Tengelmann, has used its opportunities in China, where it is successful now. In the recent months many major players have announced to try to expand strongly in the Chinese mainland. In addition, China has also some very national chains such as Lianhua, Hualian, Auchan and Wumart.[2]

There still exists a trend that was already evident in recent years. Increasingly the big retailer chains target the Chinese hinterland, which has indeed already higher growth rates than the so-called first-tier cities of the East, but still has a large backlog.[3]

Even if this trend should continue for many years, the expansion into the Chinese hinterland is a major challenge to retailers. On the one hand, the consumer needs differs in the second- and third-tier cities significantly from the habits of East Coast residents. On the other hand, the enormous logistical problems are often underestimated, that new supermarkets will face in the hinterland.[4]

Experts mention there is an opportunity for hypermarkets to penetrate China's retail sector still further by expanding into tier two and tier three cities. The hypermarket sector is a nascent industry, whose turning point is still to come as the lack of competition in second-tier cities is a chance for further development. Retailers have to act now to gain a profitable

---

[1] **Schaaf, B.** (2010).
[2] **Wesnitzer, A.** (2005).
[3] **Schaaf, B.** (2010).
[4] **Schaaf, B.** (2010).

share in the hypermarket, as local competitors are faster in developing a multi-format portfolio to diversify the business risks and capitalize other development opportunities.[1]

Overview of Wal-Mart:

Wal-Mart Stores Inc. is a global American retailing company, which dominates a large part of the U.S. market. Wal-Mart is in the list of Fortune Global 500 listed on the top of the largest companies in the world with the highest turnover. Wal-Mart has over two million employees; therefore it is the largest private employer in the world.[2]

The turnover of Wal-Mart in the year 2009 climbed from the previous year by 1% to 405.6 billion U.S. dollar. The profit rose by about 7% to 14.3 billion U.S. dollar. The company name is derived from its founder Sam Walton at (Walton's Mart). On 2 July 1962 Sam Walton opened his first Wal-Mart in Rogers (Arkansas). Ten years later, in 1972, the company went public, which gave him the necessary capital for expansion. The big rise started in 1987, when Wal-Mart opened its first supermarkets under the name Hyper Market USA. It had a department store which retail space was ten times larger than an average store.[3]

Wal-Mart has 3702 chain stores in the U.S. and has also huge representations in Mexico, Great Britain (Asquith Dairies), Japan (Seiyu), Canada and the People's Republic of China, while markets in Germany and South Korea in 2006 were abandoned. In Mexico, Wal-Mart operates through its subsidiary Walmex.[4]

The biggest competitor, the French Carrefour group is not even half as big as Wal-Mart. Eight out of ten U.S. households buy at least once a year at Wal-Mart, every week 138 million customers worldwide enter a business of the Group. Nevertheless Wal-Mart only controls eight percent of the U.S. retail market, but in many other countries, in this area the market leader have a market share of over 30%.[5]

---

[1] **Chaudhrey, R.** (2007).
[2] **Dong, J.** (2008).
[3] **Dong, J.** (2008).
[4] **Dong, J.** (2008).
[5] **Dong, J.** (2008).

Wal-Mart has a corporate culture that employees designated as equal partners of the company. Especially in the U.S this goes hand in hand with a strong anti-union policy of the company. Only 10 employees of a meat department in the eastern United States are organized in a union.[1]

In the U.S. new employees at Wal-Mart earn on average two thirds of a unionized counterparts at any other supermarket. Similarly, there are no additional services such as a supported health insurance by the company. On average, the group must replace 44% of its workforce each year, which leads to 600 000 new adjustments every year. On average, at any given time about 1,500 complaints run against Wal-Mart, mainly against violations of U.S. labor law. [2]

Wal-Mart's marketing strategy in the Chinese market:

Wal-Mart entered the Chinese market and opened its first Supercenter and Sam's Club in Shenzhen in 1996. Currently, Wal-Mart operates a number of store formats in China including Supercenters, Sam's Clubs, and Neighborhood Markets. Right now Wal-Mart has 190 units in 101 cities, and created over 50,000 job opportunities across China.[3]

Target markets:

Wal-Mart focuses on the customers that other hypermarkets seem not to take account of, therefore it can be sad that a neglected niche is targeted. Their target group are the small town shoppers. The strategy is especially effective as it achieves instant market saturation which leads to very strong loyalty. This marketing strategy also helps to stay below leading competitor's radar while Wal-Mart builds up its competitive advantages (distribution centers, etc.) that allow growing more into mainstream.[4]

---

[1] **Dong, J.** (2008).
[2] **Dong, J.** (2008).
[3] **Walmart** (2010).
[4] **Chang, F.** (2009).

5

Wal-Mart competes on price, but they also compete on time and convenience because they offer so many products customers don't have to drive to multiple stores to get what they need. They also compete on location and reputation.[1]

Wal-Mart set up a new discount chain called Trust-Mart in China. The retail shops should attract people in rural areas with low wages. At the moment Wal-Mart runs around 190 big supermarkets with average prices in the booming areas. The new concept will help Wal-Mart to reach more consumers, not only in the cities. The first supermarket will be opened in November in the city Zhangshu in the east Chinese province Jiangxi. The shops will have a simple floor made of cement and masoned walls. The products will not be presented . Wal-Mart has similar chains in Mexico and Argentina.[2]

Competitive advantages:

Wal-Mart has been enormous successfully at the US market due to a few key factors which the hypermarket also uses for the Chinese market:

Wal-Mart's key slogan is to offer the lowest prices of products in the market. On average Wal-Mart's products are around 20% cheaper than the offers of the competitors in the US.[3] In China the products have a higher price on average. As a nation, it's hard to compete with China on price and win. China is best known for its low-cost manufacturing, thanks to low wages; however, its manufacturers are starting to focus on quality as a means of increasing their competitive advantage. The best never focus their competitive strategy on price alone. They combine multiple competitive strategies to create a lasting advantage and continue to innovate as they use technology to raise the bar with each method.[4]

Wal-Mart built up a win-win partnership with their suppliers, but still acts as a very dominant negotiator. Concentrated on lower prices, Wal-Mart provides its suppliers with support and

---

[1] **Jahan, N.** (2011).
[2] **Klein, P.** (2010).
[3] **Chang, F.** (2009).
[4] **Jahan, N.** (2011).

consultancy and goes into details to achieve efficiency for their businesses, so that the suppliers achieve the aspired low prices.[1]

Wal-Mart was able to build one of the most efficient distribution systems in the US. The distribution centers are constructed so that any Wal-Mart's stores have a distribution center less than a day's drive away. Moreover the hypermarket operates its own truck fleet which has led to 99.5% on time delivery record.[2]

Wal-Mart has invested heavily in its unique cross-docking inventory system. With this system, goods are continuously delivered to stores within 48 hours and often without having to inventory them. Therefore Wal-Mart is able to replenish the shelves 4 times faster than its competitions.[3]

Challenges in China's retail market:

It was easy for Wal-Mart to enter the Chinese market, but some things just don't work effectively in China.[4] The country is not the first location Wal-Mart has been facing difficulties at, like the mentioned pullouts from South-Korea and Germany. China's retail market entails serious challenges, so that the opportunities envisioned by looking at China high growth market are undermined, such as the uprising middle class and still unexplored markets.

In China the people earn strongly different high wages, which depend on their employment, social status, province they live in, and whether they are from a rural or an urban place. Some parts of the population are very poor and might have different purchasing habits. Planning a marketing strategy this point of the diverse population has to be considered.

The retail market is exploding in China right now, so that there is a huge amount of hypermarket players. Even though foreign companies have a relatively strong liquidity and international backing, local companies have an advantage in their in-depth knowledge of the

---

[1] **Chang, F.** (2009).
[2] **Chang, F.** (2009).
[3] **Jahan, N.** (2011).
[4] **Chang, F.** (2009).

local market; therefore they adapt very quickly and establish wide spread and cheap distribution systems.[1]

The regulations set by the central government are not always followed by the local governments. There seems to be a strong local bias for local and state-owned companies and against foreign companies. State regulations against it are seldom enforced.[2]

The infrastructure is backward and costly in China. The roads still cannot keep up with modern standards and are often toll-based. The distribution from port to destination by rail is extremely slow and often requires overnight storages. Furthermore the IT communication is far behind in many areas on both speed and connectivity, especially in the hinterland.[3]

Marketing mix:

The focus that Wal-Mart shares in all advertisements is service, low prices, and quality of goods. Wal-Mart is not a specialty shop focusing on one "good", they are innovative offering a selection based on consumers overall needs. They do have some brand name merchandise however do not have a specific section set aside for Polo Shirts.[4]
In China they also offer many some products which you cannot purchase in the US like: Crocodiles, bulk rice, turtles, Wal-Mart brand spirits, rib cages, assorted dried reptiles, frogs, large selection of chopsticks, great value brand beef granules and pig faces.

[1] **Chang, F.** (2009).
[2] **Chang, F.** (2009).
[3] **Chang, F.** (2009).
[4] **Jahan, N.** (2011).

Conclusion of the performance in China:

RMB bn	Revenue	Growth (%)	Ranking
2003	5.85	-	16
2004	7.64	30.47	20
2005	9.93	30.1	22
2006	15.03	51.32	14
2007	21.32	41.8	13
2008	27.82	30.53	9
% change	375.41	-	-

Wal-Mart (China) Investment: Financial Results 2003-2008:

Wal-Mart has so far refused to reveal its sales figures for China. The only publicly available sales figures for Wal-Mart are from the China Chain Store and Franchise Association (CCFA). Wal-Mart's revenue in China excluding Trust-Mart grew by 375.41% between 2003 and 2008 to RMB27.82bn.[1]

Looking back, it seem that there are some major differences between Wal-Mart and Carrefour's strategy that contributed to Carrefour doing better in comparison to Wal-Mart. The main difference seems to be around the issue of adjusting to local culture. While Carrefour was mainly trying to localize and do things "the Chinese way" by encouraging local branch decision making, building local supplier contracts, stretching local rules and regulations, and using local promotion marketing schemes, Wal-Mart was more focused on doing things the American way – the way that made Wal-Mart was it is today in the American market. This contributed to the fact that Wal-Mart has been struggling throughout many of the difficulties described above with the local customer, government and suppliers. China is considerably different than the states and yet Wal-Mart has been slow to try to adjust to that, which just might cost Wal-Mart the entire Chinese market (as it has in Germany and South Korea).[2]

[1] **Schmidt, R.** (2009).
[2] **Jahan, N.** (2011).

Suggestions for Wal-Mart:

Wal-Mart needs to adjust to the Chinese market, while leveraging its source of competitive advantage. This requires a delicate balance. At the US, the brand Wal-Mart is associated with low price rather than quality. In China, where everyone is going for low prices and providing low quality to do so, Wal-Mart's own brand could be an assurance for low prices but with quality by making the Wal-Mart name about more than just retailing. Wal-Mart's strategy is heading in that direction. In China it is already associated with higher reliability and quality assurance.

Although Wal-Mart is a Joint-Venture, the sources do not mention any attempt to leverage the local partner to meet the local market, which seems the opposite to some other joint ventures discussed like Danone and Wahaha. Working together with the local partner to understand where and how the local regulations can be used or adjusted for Wal-Mart's success and gaining a stronger hold of the potential customer's heart might help Wal-Mart's growth and dominance in the Chinese market.[1]

Chinese consumer habits needed to be kept in mind as the Chinese consumers go shopping to get out of the house, not necessarily to shop. They're more impulse driven and like on-site promotions. They're brand conscious but not loyal. They're frequent shopper of small amounts and especially appreciate freshness (alive) due to limited space at home.[2] This seems a bit off the original Wal-Mart strategy and so Wal-Mart's needs to go deeper in trying to understand who the consumers are and what they're looking for. Following those characteristics it might be more relevant to focus on the shopping experience and salesperson fleet using aggressive promotion methods. A bigger number of smaller shops with a more of wet-market feeling might be more to the local taste than the American style shops.

Taking all these aspects into consideration it can be said that Wal-Mart does a god job in China, even though it has to face some problems. Wal-Mart is the most successful foreign

---

[1] **Jahan, N.** (2011).
[2] **Walmart** (2011).

hypermarket in China and they still expend in the country. The future might be positive affected through the establishment of the discount chain Trust-Mart.

Bibliography

Chang, F. (2009), China Business Strategy: Walmart and Chinese Culture. Online document: http://www.filination.com/blog/2009/03/14/china-business-strategy-walmart-chinese-culture/. (05.05.2011)

Chaudhrey, R. (2007), Hypermarket Culture Booms in China. Online document: http://www.talkingretail.com/news/industry-news/hypermarket-culture-booms-in-china. (01.05.2011)

Dong, J. (2008), Wal-Mart's Investment in China Hypermarket Operator to Bring New Value to China's Shoppers. Online document: http://investors.walmartstores.com/phoenix.zhtml?c=112761&p=irol-newsArticle&ID=967478&highlight=. (04.05.2011)

Jahan, N. (2011), How to win Chinese consumers: Competitive Strategy of Wal-Mart in China. Online document: http://wbiconpro.com/17[1].-Jaya.pdf. (11.05.2011)

Klein, P. (2010), Wal-Mart startet Diskounterkette in China. Online document: http://news.orf.at/stories/2028606/. (11.05.2011)

Schaaf, B. (2010), China wird zum größten Supermarkt der Welt. Online document: http://www.handelsblatt.com/unternehmen/mittelstand/china-wird-zum-groessten-supermarkt-der-welt/3418302.html?p3418302=4. (01.05.2011)

Schmidt, R.(2009), Wal-Marts finanzielle Resultate. Online document: http://handelsblatt.com/Wal-Marts-finanzielle-Resultate/21361274html.?ashdsa=. (12.05.2011)

Wesnitzer, A. (2005), Chinas Verbrauchermarkt auch von deutschen Firmen heiß umkämpft. Online document: http://www.innovations-report.de/html/berichte/studien/bericht-50096.html. (01.05.2011)

Walmart (2010), Wal-Mart China factsheet. Online document: http://www.wal-martchina.com/english/walmart/index.htm. (05.05.2011)